What Does Love Got to Do with It?

Understanding and Operating in the Power of God

by Vernadette R. Augustusel

PublishAmerica
Baltimore

© 2004 by Vernadette R. Augustusel.
All rights reserved. No part of this book may be reproduced, stored in a retrieval system or transmitted in any form or by any means without the prior written permission of the publishers, except by a reviewer who may quote brief passages in a review to be printed in a newspaper, magazine or journal.

First printing

Unless otherwise indicated, all Scripture quotations are from the Holy Bible, New International Version, by the International Bible Society. Used by permission of Zonderan Publishing House.

ISBN: 1-4137-4412-5
PUBLISHED BY PUBLISHAMERICA, LLLP
www.publishamerica.com
Baltimore

Printed in the United States of America

Dedication

In honor and loving memory of Brenda Brooks, a dear friend, who encouraged and stayed after me to minister through written material.

Also a special thanks to my family and the countless friends who prayed me through.

Table Of Contents

Introduction..07

Chapter 1..09
The Power of Love

Chapter 2..15
Lord, Teach Us How to Love

Chapter 3..20
Hello Judas, Goodbye Pain

Chapter 4..25
Danger!!! (The Absence of Self Love)

Chapter 5..29
For if They Knew Better, They Would Do Better (How to forgive when it hurts

Chapter 6..33
Show Me Your Love

Chapter 7..40
What Does Love Got to Do with It?

Prayer..45

Steps Towards Perfecting Your Love Walk..........................46

Bibliography..47

Introduction

In a ten year life span of being saved for real, God has helped me to understand and realize that our love walk is vital and very important to our spiritual development and growth. Through various relationships I've come to understand that we as Christians are not walking in love the way God has intended. Too many of us claim to be saved and have a serious relationship with God, but yet we walk in hatred, jealousy, and strife at the same time. Far too many brothers and sisters in the body of Christ are rejoicing over the failure, fall, and weakness of each other. It grieves the very heart of God to see his children not walking in sincere love toward each other, ourselves, and ultimately God our Father. Now is the time to live and operate in the kingdom of God, here on earth, since we are the sons and daughters of God. When we compete with each other instead of complement each other we are not operating in kingdom business, but rather we have seriously missed God and have now crossed over into operating in the kingdom of darkness without ever realizing it.

One day the love-walk message began to come to me as I was preparing to leave for the West Coast with my oldest son. My oldest son had just finished high school, and he had hopes of going away to a very nice school for the arts in California. However, it had never accured to me that some folks around me did not expect very much from my life and that of my children, until we landed an interview with the school and were preparing to leave. During that time we were struggling. We struggled with our son getting him through high school. Then we struggled with getting enough money for our round trip flights, car rental, and hotel. Bottom line is at one time we struggled financially. It all was a big struggle for us, but God some how, worked it all out. So why would anyone be jealous of us, instead of praying for us, was what I could not understand.

As word began to get out that we were going to California for a mini vacation and interview with a school, some of the folks around us began to act very indifferent toward us. From then on I've taken note of how some folks are happy for you and some are not when things are well with you. Jealousy came from folks who had a lot more than we did, and some had even experience being blessed in the very way were hopping to be. Nevertheless, to my surprise, some folks were not so happy to see God bless my family and me. We expected jealousy from the world, but not our brothers and sisters in Christ.

We had a wonderful time while we were away, but the love message God was birthing in me would not leave me alone. The love message would come to me every time I would come back to the room. Every time I would meditate, God's love message would not leave me alone. As I reflected on what God had birthed in me, I would pray, read, and write/journal about some of the things God was revealing to me about our love walk. Even when we got home the love message would not leave, at different times and places it would come. God used situations, circumstances, and experiences of the past to birth a message of love in me.

After that experience and many others, my heart would ache and was sore as God revealed, anointed, and appointed me to write. As one of God's dearest children I can only image how He must feel when we do not walk in His divine love.

Chapter 1

The Power of Love:

God is calling us to a radical love walk. What is love? Well according to the word of God, love is several different things. In *I Corinthians 13:4-7*, I believe we have a good picture of what true love is. "Love is patient, love is kind. It does not envy, it does not boast, it is not proud. It is not rude, it is not self-seeking, it is not easily angered, and it keeps no record of wrongs. Love does not delight in evil, but rejoice with the truth. It always protects, always trusts, always hopes, and always perseveres."

Now that we have an idea of what love is, look at what love is not: it is not manipulation, deceit, hatred, jealous, envy, strife, rebellion, discord, control, greed, betrayal, nor selfishness. Love is a spirit and the Bible says that God is love, *I John 4:8*. So that would make love alive and active, a spiritual force. And where there is love, there is the presence and power of Almighty God.

As we allow the power of God's love to flow through our lives, we can experience joy, and excitement for living. Like the old song says, "This joy that I have, the world did not give it to me and the world can not take it away." This is so true because the realization of God's love will give you joy for living, no matter what situation or circumstance you may be facing. The love of God will always bring victorious living. When one becomes aware of God's love it will bring them a sense of peace, an unexplainable sense of peace. So many people too often don't have a seal for living. They just go through life existing from one day to the next, simply because they do not realize how much God loves them, and how much He wants His love to flow in and through them.

God's love is one of the first spiritual gifts to humanity, but most of us do not acknowledge the depth of God's love simply because we don't realize that it is a spiritual force with power and anointing abilities. And because we have not acknowledged God's love, we cannot operate in God's power, and the authority He has given us on earth. What we need to do is give up our hang-ups and get together and serve God and each other in the force of love, the spirit of love. If we could just understand that when we are schematic, plotting, backbiting, and harboring jealousy and hatred towards each other, the kingdom of darkness advances. But if we learn to walk in God's love, the kingdom of heaven advances. One quick question, whose side are you on? Let's get together on kingdom business and work on bringing the kingdom of God here on earth. When we are not walking in God's love, His spiritual force, we are actually working against Him and His kingdom. Either we are for God, by walking in His love, His spirit, His force, or we are working for Satan harboring ill feelings and operating in evilness. Quick question again, whose side are you on?

The fruit of the spirit is love. A good example of walking in God's love is in *Galatians 5:22-23*. We are reminded of what these fruits are and what they will produce if we walk in them. "But the fruit of the Spirit is love, joy, peace patience, kindness, goodness, faithfulness, gentleness, and self-control." Everything in which God the Father wanted to teach us is based wholly on love, our love for Him, and our love for each other. This is also why the word of God reminds us that the greatest commandment to keep is to walk in love: *Mark 12:28-34, Matthew 22:37, Romans 13:8-10, Galatians 5:13-14.* Without love we have nothing because anything absent from love is without God. The very excess of God is exemplified in love. Everything in the kingdom is based on love and we have nothing without love, not even access to kingdom benefits and blessings. In *Mark 12:34* when Jesus was being questioned about which of the commandments was the greatest, he told the religious teachers that the greatest of all commandments is to walk in love. And believe it or not that's just where your healing is, your blessings, your peace, and your prosperity, even as your soul prospers. It's all connected to our love walk. Now, I ask you how can we say that we are for God and not walking in the fruit of the Spirit and the power of God's love? How can we say we know Him and not practice His presences? When we practice love and the other fruits of the Spirit we are actually practicing being in God's presence. The entire word of God is summed up in a single command: "Love your neighbor as yourself." (Galatians 5:14) Friend, examine your love walk. If someone is walking in hatred, envy, cheating, and greed, just to name a few, their love walk is out of order. Get back in line with God, and start practicing His presence by walking in love. So many of us miss out on the greatest love affair of a lifetime because we don't acknowledge God's love. We must examine ourselves and allow the love of God to flow in and through our lives. Oh, by the way, God plays for keeps. He is not looking for any part-time loves. So if you think of skipping out on Him and two-timing Him, it's best that you don't mess with Him in any kind of way. We need to be consumed with the love of God or leave it alone. Just as Jesus was a living example of God's love, we are to be an example also.

Our love walk is very important to our Christian walk and spiritual growth. The more of God's love we walk in the more we grow spiritually. As we walk in God's love, the evidence of His presence and power is made manifest in and through our lives. If we will allow God, His love will transform us. As more of the transformation takes place we become more like Him. God intends for us to be transformed into His image more and more. It is my belief that the more we yield to the spirit of love the more we walk in the power of God. And the power of God's love will turn our lives completely around. The word says it is the goodness of the Lord that causes us to repent. God's goodness demonstrates His love shown towards us. This love, once experienced, will cause one to become a new person in Christ Jesus. As we allow God's love to transform us, His power will flow in and through our lives to change things for the better.

Love will always affect our quality of life, how well and how long we live. Some people have literally died from a broken heart in which they felt as though no one truly loved them. Perhaps they never experienced how to love God or themselves. Sadly, they did not come to know and understand that God's love was available to them. Love is a very important part of life. As we develop, it is very important that we experience love, but most importantly we need to experience God's love. It is my belief that if someone were raised in an atmosphere of love or maybe experiencing love later on in life, they would normally have a healthy lifestyle. Healthy emotions and a sense of well being, I believe, are signs of someone experiencing love and care. Folks who have been abused emotionally, mentally, and/or physically, normally are afraid to love because they don't know if they can ever trust themselves to love. They are afraid of being hurt again. Trust is a major part of love and folks who have been hurt don't want to hurt anymore. To keep from being hurt again from the lack of love, these folks will put up different defense mechanisms to guide their hearts and feelings from being hurt. So many people today are afraid to love. They desire and want love more then anything, but they are in a prison from past experience, so they refuse to walk in love or allow themselves to be loved. These folks see no way of ever getting out from the prison of no love.

Dear friend, there is a way out and it is through Jesus Christ. Jesus is the way, the truth and the light, he came to set the captives free. As the word says whomever Jesus set free is free indeed. You may ask yourself how do I get out of the prison of no love . Well just call on the name of the Lord Jesus right where you are. Ask him for help and be truthful with Him. Tell Him that you want out and you want to love again or experience love for the very first time. Tell Him that you need to experience love and give love, but that you don't know how or where to begin. As we open ourselves to love we must understand that pain and hurt may come, but love and give love as if no one will ever hurt you again. So that God's love can flow in and through your life. We must learn to over look people's offenses because if we don't we will walk around in the bondage and pain of folks hurting us. Everyday practice overlooking the pain someone is trying to cause you. This will keep you free from the spirit of offense. In other words, learn to forgive as much as possible.

Once you are out of the prison of no love, you must make sound decisions and be determined that you are never going back behind those bars of imprisonment again. Fight for your freedom to love and be loved because it is a daily battle. Every day of your life you will be faced with the choice of holding on to the pain and hurt of the past and present or to walk in love. Sometimes others will bring you their pain and hurt, just to see or cause you pain and hurt. But reject it and show them the depth of God's love. The power of God's love can conquer all things, but we must have faith in that. The Bible tells us that it is impossible to please God without faith. Well faith in what? We must have faith in the power of God's love and the fact that it is real. If we do not exercise faith in the power of God's love it cannot and will not work for us. Each day we must make a choice to do something with pain and hurt. What are you going to do with it? Are you going to exercise your faith and release it to God or hold on to it? Will you begin each day with a commitment to walk in God's love or go back to the prison of no love? Friend, you've got to fight the good fight of faith and stay free to walk in God's love. We walk in God's love by daily communication with Him. Spend some time with Him, so that He can empower you to walk in His love. This is the only way to stay free to love God's way. To walk in God's love is to walk in the supernatural. If you try to love in your ability you will fail to love, but remember God's love is a powerful force. His love is His spirit and His presence that is alive and active, which helps or empowers us to love when love seems impossible.

We can walk in God's love and move by His power in several ways:

1. Be aware of your inner man/your spiritual man, we need to be aware of where we are spiritually. Make a daily assessment of where you are spiritually, and be truthful with yourself. If something is not right in your spirit, repent and get yourself together.
2. Be committed to daily devotions through prayer, reading, and studying the word of God. On a daily basis commune with Him. Meditate on His love for you and His promises. Listen to the word, speak and confess the word over yourself.
3. Submit and surrender all and any ill feelings you may be harboring. Cleanse your heart daily.

Psalm 51:10 tells us to ask God to create in us a clean heart and renew a right spirit within us. In order for God to pour His love in our hearts, our hearts must be cleaned out. God's love cannot come into a place filled with ill feelings and evilness. Make sure your heart is right.

4. Walk in forgiveness. Practice being kind to others. Learn to smile and learn to laugh again. Lift up your head and live again, there is always something to live for. In *Ecclesiastes 9:5* the word of God says, "As long as you are alive there is hope, it is better to be a live dog than a dead lion because the dead have no hope for living."

5. Daily cast your cares and anxieties on God the Father. *II Peter 5:7*, "Cast all your cares on Him because He cares for you." Be thankful, be joyful, and remember to pray about everything. *I Thessalonians 5:16-18*

6. Learn to trust God to help you to love the unlovable. Remember to ask Him to help you and walk in His love. Practice, practice, practice walking in love because practice makes perfect. In other words, practice brings maturity in your love walk. Never give up, always keep trying to walk in love.

7. Remember love never fails and understand that if we give love and sow love, love will find its way back to us. We always reap what we sow.

Chapter 2

Lord Teach Us How to Love:

Ephesians 3:16-19
I pray that out of his glorious riches he may strengthen you with power through his spirit in your inner being. Christ may dwell in your heart through faith. And I pray that you, being rooted and established in love, may have power and together with all the saints grasp how wide, long, high, and deep is the love of Christ; and to know this love surpasses knowledge that you may be filled to the measure of all the fullness of God.

At one time in my life, when I believed that I was walking in the God kind of love, the word of God opened up to me and revealed that I really was not as lovable as I thought. Scriptures or the word of God will help you to understand that God's ways are truly not our ways. I realized that in order for us to walk in and operate in God's love, we must first know and understand what the God kind of love is and what we have come to understand and know love to be. If we were to size ourselves up against the word of God and it's many different meanings of love, we would live in victory more than in defeat because the God kind of love never fails. *1 Corinthians 13:8.*

Too often we have come to believe that love is for weak folks and wimps, but not so. A fearless person is one who walks in love. They are not afraid to love, "For perfect love cast out fear." (I John 4:18) There are misconceptions of a person walking in love. People walking in love are not weak, fearful, timid, and push-overs. I will say this again. One of the greatest and most powerful people to ever live was Jesus Christ. He continuously walked in the God kind of love. Walking in love is not always easy either, but it is rewarding and worth it. It takes strength to walk in love. A person operating in love is someone who is courageous, and someone who has self-control. Being able to walk in love would take someone who is secure and someone who can hold their peace in the midst of confusion and trouble. A person demonstrating love is someone who can walk in forgiveness towards folks who are deliberately trying to hurt them and cause them pain. Actually, Christian love is one of the highest forms of spiritual warfare. This is why God commands and reminds us to walk in it. People operating in God's love will not wimp out under pressure. When someone mistreats a person operating in love, they won't retaliate because they know and understand that their inner man will be strengthened to operate in God's love or should I say God's power of forgiveness. (Ephesians 3:16-19) A person who walks in God's love will stand up for the truth and tell the truth in love, while knowing and believing God's love will protect them. A wimp would not and could not allow folks to strip them naked in front of their community, hang them on a cross/a tree, and kill them for something they did not do. That type of situation would take supernatural strength to handle. It would take the God kind of love. Most of us don't realize that God's love has supernatural strength to empower you with supernatural abilities. This kind of love can forgive someone who opposes you every chance they get just because they want to. This kind of love can give until it hurts to someone who is despitefully using him or her because they trust in God's love to reward them down the road.

    Love is the foundation of all things that are Godly. Without love, you have nothing and because God is love, without God you have nothing. Not only is love a spiritual force and God's presence, but also love is also a choice and an action. If we choose to walk in love, we will open up to God's spirit. When we walk in love we walk in God, His power, His characteristics, and His anointing. God showed His love to us by dying on the cross for sins He did not commit. God came down from heaven in the form of Jesus Christ and bore our sins, curses, sickness, and miserable filthy condition, so that we may have an abundant life and eventually have eternal life. Now that's love! God did not have to do that, but He chooses to because of His love for humanity and His creation.

There are three dimensions of love.

The first dimension of love is *"Agape"*. It is a Greek term that best describes the God kind of love. It is the purest form of love, which is a divine love. Agape is the gift of love God has for humanity. It is not characterized by desires, attractions, or need.

"Philia" the second dimension of love is characterized as a friendship or brotherly love, which humans desire and give each other.

Love of desire or of a sexual nature is known as *"Eros."* Eros is the third dimension of love, which is mainly physical. (Bowden, Richardson 341-342)

Not only are there three dimensions of love, but also there are several forms or types of love. When we say we love, we can mean any number of different things. A Canadian by the name of John Lee in 1973/1974 developed a widely cited approach to love. Lee suggested that there were six styles of love:

1. *Eros -Love of beauty, powerful physical attraction, and sexual desire.*
2. *Mania -Obsessive love, jealousy, possessiveness, and intense love dependency.*
3. *Ludus -Playful love, carefree quality, casualness; fun and games approach*
4. *Storge -Companionate love, peaceful and affectionate love based on mutual trust and respect.*
5. *Agape -Altruistic love, self sacrificing, kind and patient love. God's kind of love, divine love.*
6. *Pragma - Practical love, sensible, realistic.* (Benokraitis 119)

After viewing the different dimensions and types or forms of love, now let us look at what God's word says about love. In 1 *Corinthians 13:4-8*, the word says that love is patient, love is kind. It does not envy, it does not boast, it is not proud. It is not rude, it is not self-seeking, it is not easily angered, and it keeps no record of wrongs. Love does delight in evil but rejoice with the truth. It always protects, always trusts, always hopes, and always perseveres. *Love never fails.*

Wow! The love of God is really something. Now if we were to

carefully read God's definition of love and be very truthful with ourselves, we would have to admit that we all have issues to work on concerning our love walk. One day as my husband and I were really going through, we had this big argument about something stupid, in which I learned a lesson about love. I had this self-righteous approach to judging him and telling him that I knew what love was and I walked in love towards him, but that he did not walk in love towards me.

Well the very next day I went to meet him after work to continue the fight and while I was waiting for him to get off from work in my car, I began to read (I Corinthians 13), the love chapter as it is known. As I read, the word of God began to convict me of my love walk. Reading down the list of the God kind of love, I could do nothing, but repent and drive off. "Love is not easily angered, and it keeps no record of wrong." While on those two verses alone, I was busted right there. So I kindly packed my Bible up and drove home.

Our ways seem right to us, but God wants us to learn His ways of doing things. Believe it or not God is wiser and smarter than we are. His word is filled with truth and direction for our lives, if we would just submit to its authority. If we are truly wise, we will come to understand that God created us, and if there is anything we need to know about or understand we need to check in with the one who created us. Let the spirit of wisdom minister to you through reading the word and prayer. Most importantly we need to stop examining ourselves against human standards and examine ourselves (our hearts and mind) with the word of God. God sent His word to heal us and work out all unrighteousness that is in us. (Psalm 107:20) (Psalm 51:10)

Ever since that day God has been dealing with me concerning my love walk. I realized that I had to cry out to God and ask Him to teach me how to love. When we realize that we need help from God the Father, He is right there, ready and willing to assist us. So many people are able to help you but are not willing. God, however, is able and willing to help us in our love walk. The word says that He is a very present helper in our time of need. (Psalm 46:1) But are you willing and ready to obey what He has already instructed you to do and that is walk in His love. *Romans 5:5* remind us that God, "has poured out His love into our hearts by the Holy Spirit, whom He has given us."

God's help is available to assist us in our love walk, but we must be willing to cry out for help and ask Him to teach us how to walk in His love, His way. The only way we are going to be able to walk in the God kind of love is by one experience and example at a time. The perfect example has been demonstrated for us through the personhood of Jesus Christ. While we were sinners and enemies of God, Christ died for us on the cross. There is an old saying, "practice makes perfect." To practice something until it is perfect simply means to become mature in something. Well the only way God is going to teach us how to walk in His love is through practice. Everyday of our life we have a chance to practice how to walk in the God kind of love. Or are we going to continue to live and handle things like the natural man, old man, and the sinner man would handle things? The choice will always be ours.

The only way in which God is going to teach us how to love is by one experience at a time. Everyday you and I are faced with opportunities to walk in the God kind of love or to walk in our own strengths, power, and abilities. The only way we will learn to love like God is if we decide and chose to love like Him. God has not called us to be doormat for folks to just walk all over and allow ourselves to be treated any kind of way. As a child of God we have the Holy Ghost and we know when we are walking in love or not. Remember when we walk in love, we walk in God's power, and His strength because greater is He that is in us, than he that is in the world. (I John 4:4) God did not create us to be foolish people. A person who walks in the God kind of love is not foolish nor are they pushovers. Someone operating in the God kind of love can stand in a hard place with power and authority without being nasty and bitter because of the supernatural strength of God's love.

Chapter 3

Hello Judas, Goodbye Pain:

There are going to be times when we all will experience betrayal by someone very close to us. At the time of the betrayal it will be devastating and painful at first, but as time moves on we must learn to pickup what's left and continue on life's journey. During different stages of one's life someone operating in the spirit of Judas will be there lurking around pretending and trying to act as if they will be there for us, loving us, and supporting us. They are not really for us. Please note that someone with the Judas' spirit may be hanging around you, but remember he is not for you, nor is he with you. Someone operating in the Judas spirit is sent by Satan to kill, steal, destroy, and sabotage the promises, blessing, and plans of God for your life. The spirit of Judas is so deceitful and is a disruptive spirit. Some folks don't realize that they have yielded to the spirit of Judas and are operating in it towards their brothers and sisters in the body of Christ. They don't understand that they are destroying or trying to destroy someone's life. We need to understand that the spirit of Judas can only operate through someone who has yielded to demonic oppression and someone who is harboring ill feelings such as: jealousy, envy, strife, and hatred. When we are quick to release ill feelings, the Holy Spirit of the living God and the power of His love can then flow through us. The Holy Spirit tries to reveal things to us when there is something off in our spirits that we need to address. Yielding to Satan and his counsel, however, allows and opens the door to ill feelings like the spirit of Judas, which take root and grow in our spirits. Just as love is a spiritual force that God uses to empower us, Judas is also a spiritual force that the enemy uses to destroy many lives. A lot of times Judas will try to go with us to the next level and stop the move of God in our lives, but he cannot. Hatred, deceitfulness, and any kind of evilness cannot stand to be around when promotion to the next level is happening for you. Remember promotion does not come from the east, the west, or the south, but true promotion comes from the Lord. *Psalm 75:7-6* Wherever the Lord is, there is the presence of love because God is love. God loves us so much that he desires to promote us from where we are to another level in Him. For God desire that we be in health and wealth, even as our very souls proper. Now that's promotion in every area of life. *III John 1:2*

Love is again a powerful force, a spiritual force that brings promotion. The spirit of love is the actual presence of God, just as ill feelings and every form of evilness is the presence of demonic forces. Wherever God's love is in action, the presence of evil cannot be there because they cannot coexist. God's love always brings promotion and evilness brings destruction. In His love we move from glory to glory. *(II Corinthians 3:18)* In God we are to be moving from glory to glory. Jesus was our perfect example because he demonstrated in the flesh what we are suppose to be doing. As the glory of God moved in Jesus' life, his promotion was at hand, and some of the Jewish leaders desired to kill him. The Jewish leaders had these ill feelings because they had the spirit of Judas.

Please note, you don't have to spend time worrying and trying to figure out who is the Judas in you life because the power of God's love will always reveal and expose who is for you and who is not. Love is a spirit, and the word of God tells us in *I John* that God is love. So there is nothing hidden from the spirit of God and the power of God's love. Let us look at the encounter between Jesus and Judas right before the ultimate betrayal. In *John 13:21* Jesus spirit was troubled and he says to the disciples seated around him. "I tell you the truth, one of you is going to betray me." Jesus knew whom and when his betrayal would happen because of the power of God's love flowing through him had revealed it to him. Even in the midst of what was about to happen Jesus operated in love towards Judas. He did not try to harm or hurt Judas in anyway. We must understand that revenge belongs to God. Too often we waste time and energy trying to hurt folks and get back at them for the wrong they have done to us. *John 13:27* says that Jesus looks at Judas and tells him to do what ever he has to do quickly. Jesus was able to operate in power because he kept himself available and open to God's love. He did not allow Judas to steal his focus off of what God was calling him to do. Once Judas is revealed to you, don't allow him to steal your focus. Stay focused on what you have to do and keep going. Don't stop to fight with Judas because he cannot stop the promotion of God in your life. "If God be for you who can be against you," *Rome 8:31*. We have to know that God is for us. As a matter of fact, God is so much for promoting His children that he will even use Judas to help promote them from one level to the next.

Look at the story of Joseph and his brothers and how they hated him so bad that they sought to kill him. They thought they were hurting him, but actually they helped in the plan of God for his life. At the end of the book of *Genesis 50:19-20,* Joseph tells his brothers not to be scared, what you meant to hurt me with, God used it to prepare me and bless me so that I might be a blessing to you all. It is so awesome how God turned all that hatred and negativity around for one man. That is just what can happen for you. God can take what folks meant to hurt us with and turn it around to bless many, but we must let the power of God's love have its way in our lives. Don't retaliate, don't try to get folks back who lie to you and who try to hurt and destroy you. Learn to trust in God's love and leave them in His hands.

Jesus felt pain and hurt just like we feel. The word says we have a high priest that went through the same things we go through, but he sinned not. (Hebrews 4:15) Jesus was truthful with himself, the inner man, that's why he could walk in forgiveness. The forgiveness Jesus walked in kept his spirit-man clean of ill feelings, ill emotions, and ill spirits so that the love of God and the power of God could flow through him. We cannot harbor ill feelings, emotions, and spirits and expect a major move of God on our behalf. The Holy Spirit, the spirit of the living God on the inside of us is very sensitive to any ill feelings, emotions, pains, and hurts. And when we harbor ill spirits it affects our love walk. Learn to examine yourself daily of any ill spirits and repent. Get yourself together so that God's love may flow through you. Be truthful with God, release and submit all illnesses in the spirit to Him, so that He can replace it with His love and His peace.

Jesus was able to move on because he did not allow himself to get stuck in the Judas experience. The most important thing we can learn from Jesus here is that he doesn't get stuck in the Judas experience. At one point we will have to decide if we are going to continue on or if we are going to die with a dead relationship and get stuck there in the Judas experience. Let's face it, some folks are in our life for a particular reason, and some are there for only a particular season. We mess up when we try to hold on to something or someone when it is time to move on in our life journey. If we are moving towards the perfect will of God, we must realize that we are on a journey heading somewhere. In the midst of our journey heading somewhere, we will experience different things and different people. God created you and I for a particular purpose and plan in life. On the journey of life, we will encounter all types of things: roadblocks, detour, traffic jams, wrong directions, accidents, and all types of road troubles, problems and people. However, that should not stop us from our journey because the word of God reminds us that if God is for us who can be against us. God is for you, and His love is waiting to empower you for your life journey. So you don't have to be afraid or be fretful of whom Judas may be in your life because God's love will protect you and see you through your journey. We must understand and realize that no weapon formed against us shall prosper, and we will refute every tongue that accuses us. (Isaiah 54:17) As a matter of fact, after Judas has been exposed to you and the betrayal has been committed against you, start looking for a promotion. Your promotion will be in the spiritual realm or natural, and a lot of times both because the word tells us that we can have health and wealth even as our souls prosper, *III John 1:3*. God will give you double for your trouble if you are willing to move on in the spirit of love. (Isaiah 61:7)

After an encounter with Judas, if we ever would learn the art of forgiveness our healing process would happen quicker than we could imagine. If we ever learn to release folks from the pain, insults, and injuries they caused us, we could move on with our lives for the better. So many of us are looking for Judas to come to us and ask us to forgive them, but most times it will never happen. And in some cases it cannot happen for several reasons, due to a death, or perhaps relocation. Sometimes it's just not in them to acknowledge that they have wronged you. However, at any rate it is very important for us to be healed. In such cases as this, we must rely on and turn to God for healing. Also during those times it is very important to release the pain, the hurt, and move on with our lives. Our healing, soundness, and wholeness should not be in the hands of Judas anyway because he comes to destroy. Stop giving Judas the power to heal you. He can't. It's impossible for him. He is a destroyer. He is on the enemy's side to destroy us. Some healing is supernatural and only God can heal certain places in our lives. And believe me, God knows and He is waiting and wanting to help and heal us, but we must acknowledge and turn to Him. God knows all about it. In *Genesis 29:31* only God could heal Leah, "When the Lord saw that Leah was not love, he opened her womb." When love hurts, what do you do? Turn to God for a supernatural healing. In the midst of the Judas experiences God will see our pain and do something very special for us, but we must turn from the pain to a healing, and loving God to receive it. When we say, "Hello Judas, I forgive you," the love of God comes in and says, "Goodbye" to the pain. Once we say goodbye to the pain we can say welcome to a glorious future. Which one do you want? We can't have both. While reaching for our healing we must let go of the pain. If we hold to the pain, we can't embrace our healing. The choice is ours, and God will not make the decision for us. We have the will to choose. God has set before us two open doors, which one will you choose, blessings or curses, Judas and pain or healing and blessings? The choice is yours. *Deuteronomy 30:19-20*

Chapter 4

Danger!!!
The Absence of Self Love:

Leviticus 19:18
"Do not seek revenge or bear a grudge against one of your people, but love your neighbor as yourself. I am the Lord."

Matthew 22:39
"Love your neighbor as yourself."

Our society has major problems and much hurt because it is filled with folks who cannot love one another. They cannot love others because they don't love themselves. The truth of the matter is folks don't know how to love others, nor do they know how to practice self-love. If we knew how to practice self-love and self-care we could in turn love others as we love ourselves. Of course we do have a lot of selfish people in the world who are just concerned about themselves and their needs. Just because someone is selfish or self-centered does not necessarily mean that they love themselves. Self-love goes much deeper than just getting what one wants or desires to satisfy the natural man; and it goes deeper than just having one's own way. For we know that selfishness is not of God. Selfishness is not one of the fruits of the spirit, listed in *Galatians 5:20*. Actually to be selfish is for one to oppose the nature of God. That's arrogant to oppose the very thing that created you. To be selfish according to Webster is to be "concerned only or primarily with oneself without regard for others." Now according to this definition, a selfish person cannot love their neighbor as themselves. It would be impossible because a selfish person has no regard for anyone but himself or herself. So selfishness is not and does not represent self-love. For this reason most of us have been taught that self-love is wrong. Self-love is not wrong, but selfishness is.

However, true love, the God kind of love, does not insist on having its own way. True love for self is actually being aware of the creator and who He created them to be. This person is aware of their strength, as well as their weakness, and all in between. They will accept the good, the bad, and the uniqueness about themselves. They will deal with it most times positively. If this type of person finds himself or herself struggling with any issue concerning them, they are quick to seek the one who created them for help in that area. They are constantly going down to the potter's house for Him to work on them. (Jeremiah 18:3) For all of us is a work in progress. God took pleasure in creating us, now let Him take pleasure in shaping your life. "For I am fearfully and wonderfully made," the Psalmist says. (Psalm 139:14) You were fearfully and wonderfully made.

God the Father commanded that we love ourselves as we love others. Most of us do not realize how often we break this commandment, "love thy neighbor as you love yourself." Most of us work on loving others, but we overlook this very important part of scripture: "love thou self". When we do not love ourselves it is a slap in God's face because He said that you are fearfully and wonderfully made. God the Father took pleasure in creating us. Too often we allow society and others tell us what is beautiful and what is acceptable. Friend, what does God say about you, that is what you need to be concerned with. If we are going to be empowered we must start loving ourselves through the eyes of God and His word. It will change your life. God does not care if we are fat, skinny, short, tall, rich, poor, yellow, brown, male, female, hairy, bald, blind, cripple, or crazy. When we do not practice self-love, and when we do not accept who we really are, we are telling the God of the universe, who created everything and know all things that we know what is best. That, my friend, is a dangerous place to be because it is a form of pride. God knew what He was doing when He created you just the way you are.

Believe it or not when we constantly focus on ourselves, what's right or wrong with us, we are practicing idolatry. Danger!!! Danger!!! There we go again breaking a major rule. Stop right where you are and began to just thank God for giving you life because God could have let another seed be born instead of you. Life is always something good to thank God for. God said everything He made was good. Begin to accept who you really are, practice self-love because God tells us that He knows the plans He has for us, and the purpose and the reason of why He created us. "For I know the thoughts that I think towards you, saith the Lord, thoughts of peace, and not of evil, to give you an expected end and a future." (Jeremiah 29:11)

A person who's operating in self-love will seek God, and pursue God to find out why and for what purpose did He create them. Stop going to everyone trying to figure out why were you created. Only God really knows why you were created. God wants to reveal to you who you are, but you must seek Him through prayer and through meditating the word. God sometimes will send someone to confirm what He has already revealed to you, but so often we don't hear the voice of God because we are looking and listening to everyone else for answers. A person not practicing self-love is one who will spend their entire life trying to do and be something they where not created to be. Then the spirit of pride comes in and that same person now will wear himself or herself out trying to impress folks they don't even like, nor care for. And what is all this for except to project a false image. My friend, be real and get a life. If you love yourself you cannot be a person that is living a lie. If you love yourself be truthful with yourself and be truthful with your God. Lies cannot exist in true love. When someone is living a lie, they cannot rejoice in the truth of God. Love rejoices in the truth. And God is truth, He cannot lie. God is also love and lies cannot coexist with love. "God has said that He is not a man that He shall lie, has He not spoken and it come to pass." (Numbers 23:19) If a person does not have self-love they cannot rejoice in the truth of God. Therefore anyone who does not have self-love is someone who will live a miserable life. And a miserable life is a life absent of God, the one who created them out of love.

A person who has no self-love is one who has lived life as an impostor, hurting folks, and causing pain to everyone they come in contact with. At this point it is impossible for someone to love their neighbor as themselves because they don't love themselves. They do not know what love is. In order to give love one must know what it is. And if you don't love yourself you will not love others. Get to know yourself, you may just come to love yourself. For so many people it is difficult and hard to accept and deal with things concerning themselves, but with God's love they can do it. The worst thing for any of us to do is to avoid things we don't necessarily like about ourselves. We don't realize that to avoid something does not make it go away. To avoid something is a sign of fear, "but God did not give us a spirit of fear, but of power, love and a sound mind." (II Timothy 1:7) For the word of God reminds us that perfect love, the God kind of love cast out fear. (I John 4:18) We have nothing to fear about ourselves. Face it with the help of God the Father. It's ok to practice self-love through the eyes of God. Ask God to help you to be true to yourself and deal with what you are trying to avoid. If you seek His help, He will help you because He created you out of love. Remember what the word says in *I Peter 5:7,* "Cast all your cares on Him for He cares for you."

Chapter 5

For if They Knew Better, They Would Do Better
(How to forgive and love when it hurts):

Luke 23:32 - 34, 41
Two other men, both criminals, were also let out with him to be executed. When they came to the place called the Skull, there they crucified him, along with the criminals-one on his right, the other on his left. Jesus said, "Father, forgive them, for they don't know what they are doing." (v. 41) We are punished justly, for we are getting what our deeds deserve. But this man has done nothing wrong.

How did Jesus deal with forgiveness? And how are we going to deal with forgiveness? Jesus came to those that were his own, but his own received him not. Suffering at its worst, Jesus knew as long as we live we to will experience various hurts, pains, and sufferings. Living in a world filled with classicism, racism, and sexism we too will come to know about suffering. In our society there are a lot of "schism and isisms" going on. If there was anyone who knew what rejection and suffering was, it was Jesus. If anybody could understand what some of us felt like from time to time, it was Jesus. If there was anybody who had suffered for righteousness, peace and love, it was Jesus. If there was anybody who has ever experienced pain by the hand of someone who was crazy, selfish, jealous, mean, bitter, nasty, hateful, and just down right demonic, it was Jesus. I contend that Jesus knew how to forgive folks because first of all, he knew his Heavenly Father. He knew how to take the pain and keep on keeping on because he talked with his Father daily. Jesus also knew how to forgive his accusers and his abuser because he knew who he was, his purpose, and his destiny. Jesus knew about true love, the God kind of love, for he had come from love to give love.

Jesus also knew that the death he had to die on the cross was not going to be eternal. When Jesus was on his way to die on the cross, he did not do like so many of us, complain, fuss, and grumble. Why, because he knew that his crucifixion was not his end. He knew that his job was not yet finished. He knew that a dying world needed salvation and the only way that would happen would be through him giving up his life for so many. In the act of love what have you given up for the sake of the body of Christ? Friend, we have not truly walked in love until we have scarified something of value for the sake of someone else. "God so loved the world that He gave His only begotten son that whosoever believeth in Him should not perish, but have eternal life." (John 3:16) And the world asks, what does love got to do with it, everything my friend. If it had not been for God's love shown us, all of us would spend eternity in hell. So my friend your very life has to do with love.

In order for Jesus to walk in the God kind of love he knew he had to die from the disease called "Me, Myself, and I." This disease comes from being selfish, but Jesus was not selfish. As he walked to his crucifixion he was really already dead. You can't kill a dead man. One of the biggest reasons why so many of us cannot and will not walk in love is because we have not died to ourselves. A lot of us need to die from selfishness. I'm not talking about self-love because that is different from selfishness. A selfish person has no regards for others. Selfishness is not of God, but God however, commands us to love ourselves as we love others. Jesus was a dead man walking to be crucified. He had already died in the garden when he was praying and seeking the Father. Jesus had to do the will of his Father and that is why he knew he had to die in his likes, his dislikes, his wants, his desires, and his needs. It is in prayer that we die in the things that pull us away from God and the will of God for our lives. Prayer and meditating the word helps us to walk in the God kind of love. God's love is a supernatural kind of love, and we must seek Him to attain it. Jesus prayed and he cried, "Father if you are willing take this cup from me; yet not my will be done, but thou will be done." Every now and then we to need to pray and cry out to God the Father and ask Him for help with doing His will.

Suffering is a part of the process. The process of life. The word of God says that Jesus learned obedience through the things he suffered. (Hebrews 5:8) Suffering has its purpose. None of us look forward to it, but with God's love empowering us even suffering at its worst cannot destroy us. We are at our great point of development and empowerment when we can walk in God's love in the mist of suffering. None of us like suffering because it's unpleasant at the time, but if we just walk in God's love, it will strength us till we come to see and understand the purpose of the pain. If we continue to walk in God's love even pain will have a clear purpose in the process of our lives.

Not only did Jesus take the pain and died to himself, but he knew how to pray and go away to spend some time with his Heavenly Father. When you walk in the God kind of love you can pray for those who have wronged and hurt you. One of the things I've learned is that when people mistreat someone and operate in a manner of evil, what they are really revealing about themselves is that they do not know God. As well as they do not believe nor do they know His word and His love as they should. Just as Jesus said, "Father forgive them for they know not what they do." Believe it or not if they knew better they would do better. Folks who have a serious relationship with God the Father know how to treat people. How can we love God, who we have not seen, and not love people we see everyday because throughout the word of God we are commanded to love each other. Whoever loves God must love his brother. (1 John 4:19-21) At certain times when I find it hard to walk in love towards someone, a statement I heard many years ago comes to mind. I don't know who or where I heard it, but it has stuck with me every since. "We love Jesus Christ and God as much as the person we love the least." That one statement helps me to walk in forgiveness and the power of God's healing love.

Today our society is filled with a lot of religious folk who don't know how to treat each other. I call them the modern day Pharisees and Sadersees. They just have a form of godliness, but they deny the power of God's love to operate in and through them. As Jesus prayed, Father, forgive them for they don't realize that whatever a man swath—that shall he reap. Father, they don't understand that if they sow deceit, they shall reap deceit. Father, forgive them for they don't realize that if they tear down someone's reputation—their stuff will be torn down. Father, forgive them for they don't realize that if they plot, scheme, backbite, and connive, someone will do the same to them. Father, Father, forgive them for they don't know how to walk in your love yet.

If the truth where told a lot of us have not experienced the power of God's love because we have not yet walk in loving ourselves. Most of us spend time looking for love, but we have not given it out of the reservoir of love that God Himself has place in each of us. Ask yourself this one question, what kind of seeds have I been sowing? Have you been sowing seeds of love? Or have you been sowing bad seeds of jealousy, hatred, strife, and deceit while looking for the power of God's love? If you have not been walking in the God kind of love ask your Heavenly Father to forgive you because you did not know any better. Seek God's love and begin right where you are to operate in it. Help is available for you, just cry out to the Father for help and He will pour His love in your heart. For the word reminds us that God's love is also a hope that will not disappoint us. Those of us who decide to walk in God's love will not be disappointed. And when we have faith in His love we will not be put to shame. To have faith in God's love is to make a decision to walk in it no matter what because God can be trusted. (Romans 5:5) The Lord reminds us to continue in his love and we can do that even when folks hurt us and mistreat us, if we refuse to treat them the same way they treat us. Things will and can begin to turn around for you.

Chapter 6

Show Me Your Love:

Deuteronomy 6:5
"And thou shall love the Lord thy God with all thou heart, and with all thy soul, and with all thy might."

Matthew 22:37-38
"Jesus said unto him, thou shall love the Lord thy God with all thy heart, and with all thy soul, and with all thy mind."

The Hebrew word for love in the original is, (BH) transliterated into (Ahab), meaning—beloved, love, lovely, lover(s), dearly love, loved, loves, show your love, shows love.

Too often we tell God that we love Him and how much we really care for Him. However, there are going to be times in our lives when God is going to confront us with the spirit of truth, the inner witness, and ask us to prove our love for Him. "Prove it," the spirit of the Lord will say like any lover will say from time to time. Lately, have you demonstrated your love for God? And if so, how? Is there any proof in your daily life that you love the Lord? Bless God if you have acknowledged your love and honor for God. However, I pray for those who have not come to understand the importance of expressing their love for God. Sadly to say some of us will continue to ignore the yearning or the desire of God's request for love. Just like any lover will from time to time confront the one claiming to love them with a request of proof or the demonstration of their love for them. Remember love is a spiritual force that comes through a decision and an action. If we love someone, we will show it. To say you love someone and never show it is no validation of your love for him or her.

The word of God lets us know and understand that God desires for us to demonstrate our love for Him. *Ephesians 5:10* say, "Find out what pleases the Lord." We get so caught up in trying to please everyone else around us rather than the one who created us. In order for us to show God that we love Him we must find out what pleases Him. The same as if we were to find out what pleases the people in our lives that we love, we must do the same for God the Father. What makes them smile? What makes them happy or sad? What displeases them? Well friend, God wants that same type of attention and affection from us. We need to find out from God what makes Him happy and joyful with us and what makes Him displeased with us. If we are in tune with our inner man, the Holy Spirit, he will always let us know what pleases God.

(1 Corinthians 2:6-16) The inner witness, the spirit of God on the inside of us, tells us what He likes and dislikes. As a matter of fact if we were to study the word of God we would find out most of it. Take for instance in *Proverbs 6:16* there are six things that God says He hates and seven of them are an abomination to Him. Most of us don't know what they are nor are we trying to find out. The word of God is loaded with things that God dislikes and what He likes, but we don't spend any time trying to find out. *I Thessalonians* tell us to be joyful, pray always, and thank God in everything in Christ Jesus because this is God's will for everyone. Unless we spend time with God and His word, we will not know Him or His will for us. So how can we claim to love Him if we are not seeking to please Him.

Prove it, Where is Your Love

Deuteronomy 6:5 and *Matthew 22:37-38*, "Love the Lord your God with all our heart, and with all your soul, and with all your strength." According to this text Christians failed to love God the Father with all of their heart, soul, and strength. In other words, I believe the text is saying that we should love the Lord God with our spirit man, which represents our heart and our minds, by meditating and thinking on His word, His goodness, and His loving kindness. Love God with all our soul, which is our action, our will, our emotion, and our intellect. And we should love God with our strength, which represents our talents, and our gifts that He has blessed us with. Basically we need to love God the Father with everything we have within the spiritual realm and the natural. If we love God in the spiritual realm it will cause the natural realm, our natural man to submit to loving God. When we totally love

God with everything, I believe we will not go wrong. He wants top priority in our lives. If we were to put God first in every area of our lives, we would live victoriously and succeed in life because we would best understand how and why we were created.

So many of us go wrong because we neglect to show or demonstrate our love for God the Father. We allow so many things to replace our affection and attention for God. God tells us that He is a jealous God in *Exodus 20: 5*. We make God out of a jealous lover. Yes, jealousy is evil and wrong, and how can a good God become jealous? God has every right to become jealous over us because He created us, He knows us, and He wants what is best for us. He loves us more than we could possible love ourselves. God's jealousy is justified through His love for us. The type of jealousy that God has is not the same as if we would have. A person operating in any form of jealousy has evil intention and motives behind their feelings of jealousy. They don't want what is best for the person of whom they are jealous. But not God, for it is His desire that we have the best possible life we can have with Him at the center of it. In *John 10:10* Jesus tells is that He came that we may have life and have it more abundantly.

We should have no other God before the one and only true and living God. We are so quick to make gods out of other people like husbands, children, and friends. We make gods out of our careers, ministries, hobbies and our education. Sometimes we even make gods out of things like houses, cars, money, and clothing. In *Matthew 10:37* Jesus says, "Anyone who loves his father or mother more than me is not worthy of me; anyone who loves his son or daughter more than me is not worthy of me." None of those things or no one can ever give us what God can give us, every time the enjoyment of having things last momentarily, then we are off seeking enjoyment and pleasure in something new. Most times, we as humans are rarely satisfied and never contempt with what we have. There is nothing wrong with having things, enjoying nice and beautiful things, but to replace them with our love for the Heavenly Father is backwards. God said that He gave us all things to richly enjoy, but not to replace Him. (1 Timothy 6:17)

Religious folks don't have or possess the love of God, they just have a form of godliness. They denied the power (love) of Christ within their very souls. We are living in the last days where people will love money, themselves, and pleasure rather than love God (II Timothy 3:1-5). Even among the brothers and sister in Christ we find that folks don't really have the God kind of love for one another the way in which they should. And so the question becomes are you a saint or are you just religious? Because the saints of God possesses the love of God and they walk in it regardless of situation and circumstances or what's going on around them. The word of God says that one example of the evidence of one being a Christian is someone possessing the God kind of love. People and things are not suppose to replace our love, our attention, and affection for God. It hurts God and grieves Him when we put people and things before Him. Sometimes we lose our way and forget how much God really loves us. God desires to be intimate with us. He is the lover of our soul (Psalm 42:1). Just as the deer pants after water, He wants our soul to thirst for more of Him. And as we thirst for more of Him, in turn we began to desire to give God more of ourselves. He desires that we demonstrate our love towards Him. "Ahab," means lover in Hebrew. It is an intimate kind of love, where two become one. God desires a love relationship with us in which He will come in and be one with us just as He and Jesus are one, and just as a husband and wife become one (John 17:20-21).

Sharing the Gospel

One of the most important ways in which we show or demonstrate our love for God is by sharing the Gospel with others and by caring for others. *John 21:15-17* tells us of the last time in which Jesus appeared to the disciples. After he finished dinning on the beach with them he turns right to Simon Peter, the one who really claimed to have loved him, and begins to question his love for him. Just as we would do perhaps after a nice dinner or beautiful time with our lover we ask them if they really love us. Jesus turns to Peter and says, "Do you love me?"

"Yes, I love you Jesus," Peter answers.

A second time Jesus looks Peter straight in the eyes and says, "Do you love me, Peter?"

"Of course I love you Jesus, you know that I do."

"Then take care of my sheep," Jesus says.

Not only does Jesus want us to tell folks about him and the Father, He wants us to be kind and affectionate to each other, showing brotherly love to each other. That is how we demonstrate our love for God the Father.

A third time Jesus looks at Pete very seriously and says, "Do you love me?"

Peter is now offended because Jesus has asked him in front of the others, and Peter feels as if he's on the spot. Jesus finally responds to Peter and says again, "Feed my sheep. In other words tell folks about my Father and me. Peter share your faith and demonstrate your love for me and evangelize."

When we love someone we will tell everybody we come in contact with about him or her. Just for one minute think of your first love and how you told everybody about them. We told our friends at school and the people at work. Some of us were so in love we even told our enemies who we loved. Who have you told about Jesus lately?

Caring for Others

In *Matthew 25:35-40* Jesus describes how we demonstrate our love for the Father by caring for others. If we possess God's love you will care for others. This text is plain and simple of how we are to minister the love of God. The word says, "For I was hungry and you gave me food; I was thirsty and you gave me drink; I was a stranger and you took me in; I was naked and you clothed me; I was sick and you visited me; I was in prison and you came to me. Then the righteous will answer Him, saying, 'Lord, when did we see you hungry and feed you, or thirsty and give you drink? When did we see you as a stranger and take you in, or naked and clothe you? Or when did we see you sick, or in prison, and come to you?' And the King will answer and say to them, 'Assuredly, I say to you, in as much as you did it to one of the least of these my brethren, you did it to me.'"

Too often we as Christians talk a lot about how much we love the Lord. We want to serve Him, but when it comes time to demonstrate our love for God in how we care for those less fortunate then us, we miss the mark. Now we cannot care for the needs of everyone around us or those we come in contact with, but we can help somebody some of the time. Jesus did say we would always have the poor with us. Needy people and those less fortunate than us will always exist, but again we can make a different with the power of God's love for the betterment in someone's life. Believe it or not there are people who do not know or can't comprehend the extent of God's love for them. And it's sad to say some will never come to know God's love, His grace, and His mercy, simply because no one has taken the time to share and care for them. Friend, don't be guilty of not caring for those less fortunate. Make it your duty to care for them. *Hebrews 6:10* says that God will not forget the love you have shown His people. Stop showing favoritism towards those who have position, titles, and possessions. Don't just do things for those who can do something for you because that's really not true love. Minister the love of God to everyone. Everybody is somebody in the eyes of God because we are all of His creation and everything God made He said that it was good. One day we will be held accountable for how we cared for others and demonstrated God's love.

Critical Love
The word of God also tells us of a critical view of demonstrating our love for God by keeping his commandments. "If you love me keep my commandments." (John 14:15) This is one of the major areas where we neglect to demonstrate our love for God. "If ye keep my commandments ye shall abide in my love; even as I kept my Father's commandments, and abide in His love." (John 15:10) Holy living is a high form of demonstrating our love for God. Friend, God is just like any good lover. He tells us how to love Him. We show our love for Him by keeping His commandments and by abiding in His presences daily and as often as possible. Not only does God tell us how to love Him, He will help us to love Him. Our heavenly Father knows the days in which we live and He is waiting to helps us in our love walk towards Him,

towards others and towards ourselves. Practice his presences today by walking in His love. If you need power, blessings, and joy, walk in God's love. As we walk in God's love, joy, blessings, and power will manifest itself in our lives daily.

1 John 2:3-6
Matthew 25:35-40
Matthew 10:42
Psalm 122:1
1 John 3:4-10
Matthew 22:37-39
1 John 14:21
Hebrews 6:10
John 13:34-35
John 15:9-10, 14
John 21:15 -17
Mark 12:28-34
Romans 13:8-10
Galatians 5:13-14
1 Corinthians 13
1 John 4

Chapter 7

What Does Love Got to Do with It?

1 Corinthians 13:1-8
If I speak in the tongues of men and of angels, but have not love, I am only a resounding gong or a clanging cymbal. If I have the gift of prophecy and can fathom all mysteries and all knowledge, and if I have a faith that can move mountains, but have not love, I am nothing. If I give all I possess to the poor and surrender my body to the flames, but have not love, I gain nothing. Love is patient, love is kind. It does not envy, it does not boast, it is not proud. It is not rude, it is not self-seeking, it is not easily angered, and it keeps no record of wrongs. Love does not delight in evil, but rejoice with the truth. It always protects, always trusts, always hopes, and always perseveres. Love never fails.

John 15:9-17
As the Father has loved me, so have I loved you. Now remain in my love. If you obey my commands, you will remain in my love, just as I have obeyed my Father's commands and remain in his love. I have told you this so that my joy may be in you and that your joy may be complete. My command is this: Love each other as I have loved you. Greater love has no one than this that he lay down his life for his friends. You are my friends if you do what I command. I no longer call you servants, because a servant does not know his master's business. Instead, I have called you friends, for everything that I learned from my father I have made known to you. You did not choose me, but I chose you and appointed you to go and bear fruit—fruit that will last. Then the Father will give you whatever you ask in my name. This is my command: Love each other.

Not long ago there was a popular rock and roll song out by Tina Turner, titled, "What's Love Got to Do with It." Most of us were clear that this song was written as a result of the abuse Tina suffered from her ex-husband (Ike Turner). She suffered emotional, verbal, mental, and extreme physical abuse. On several occasions he had almost killed her. Tina, however, was able to survive and move on with her life. Also I'm very clear that it was God's love that brought Tina through the whole ordeal with her ex-husband. She had to reached deep down and tap into God's love in order to have survived what she did and to continue on with her calling and purpose in life. God's love was the supernatural power or empowerment for Tina to continue on with life.

Our focus here in the text (John 15:16), God reminds us of the fact that we did not choose Him, but that He has chosen us. And then on the same breath he reminds us of the commandment to love each other. Why? Why in the mist of him calling and choosing us for a particular reason would he reminds us to love one another? I believe He is reminding us of His love that He has placed in us so that we can possess the power to do what He created us for. If we are going to live the life that God the Father has planed for us and if we are going to bear fruit, good fruit that will last, then we must possess the spirit of love. Why the spirit of love you ask, and not some other gifts of the spirit like courage, for instance. Simple, because the spirit of love is the evidence of God's presence in us. In (I John 4:7-8), the word clearly states that God is love. Now remember love is not weak, but love is all powerful and it never fails. Why does something like love never fail? Because love is God and God is love, and God never fails. *1 Corinthians 13:1-8*

This is why some folks can operate in love towards folks who have deeply hurt them because of God's love in them. God's love is God's power or let's say God's empowerment. I disagree with sister Tina, that love is a "second-hand emotion." She sang out of her pain and the abuse she went through, but I understand why she sang the song the way she did. Her healing process was not finished, or perhaps she was reflecting upon the pain she once experienced. Sometimes it's very hard to love when we relive the pain of the past. When folks operate out of pain and hurt I believe it is a signal that they are not fully healed, and they are still hurting. Healing is a process, and for some folks it will take a lifetime to be healed. The timing of healing is not the same for everyone. However, I believe that if we allow God's love to flow through us and in us, our healing process would be a lot quicker.

For most of us we have been abused, mistreated, hurt, and sometimes left for dead. I've heard folks say, "hurting people will hurt people." I've come to believe that this is true. But if we hold on to hope somewhere in our lives the power of God's love will come and rescue us. Some of us have literally been rescued or are being rescued from the dead, maybe not a physical death, but perhaps an emotional or spiritual death. There is so much in the world that is designed to kill us spiritually, emotionally, and mentally, but if we allow God's love and power to come in, it can revive us to want to live again. Love is an anointing, an empowerment, a spiritual force of God that empowers you and helps you to do whatever you got to do. Again love is God. The spirit of love is the actual presence of God. God's love empowers you to forgive when forgiveness is really impossible and out of the question. This kind of empowerment will step in and rescue you from your darkest days and show you a way out when there is none. As a matter of fact, if God needs to His love is so powerful it can create a way out when there is no way out, just for you. Throughout the Bible we see the power of love. And there is power in His love, but unfortunately most of us do not seek it or operate in it because we do not believe in the power of love and that it will never fail us. Unfortunately, we try to figure out things on our own strength and that is where we fall short of the empowerment to live a life filled with love.

Too often and too many times we do not allow the spirit of love, the empowerment of God to come in, minister to us, and work through us. From day in and day out we go through life struggling, trying to make it on our own strength instead of operating in His love. Some of us don't even realize that we are carrying around in us, pain, resentment, bitterness, and hatred; rather than abiding in God and letting His love, His spirit, and His power abide in and through us. Sometimes abiding in God is a matter of just simply calling and crying out to Him in truth. After crying out to God, the spirit of truth will come to speak, listen. The Holy Spirit will speak and reveal to you something that is going on with you. Stop avoiding the Spirit of truth and deal with what He is trying to tell you. When He comes don't ignore him and deny the truth because He speaks for God. Tell your heavenly Father where the pain is, tell Him how they did you, and tell Him your hopes and dreams. Tell Him how you really feel, and then ask Him to help you. And then let Him help you. Stop asking God for help, and then go back to your old way of doing things. When the struggles of life come don't be bitter, nasty, critical, and mean. Walk in God's love because it is available to you. Love will keep you when you cannot be kept. Love will bless you right where you need to be blessed. God's love will strengthen you where you need to be strengthened. Love can open doors no man can shut. God's love is our divine helper and healer, that is why Jesus reminds us of how much he loves us and to remain in his love. Jesus also tells us throughout the Scripture that if we will acknowledge God the Father and His power, that God's unfailing love is available to empower and help us. We must remember that if we have not love, the word says we have nothing.

God dose not care how anointed we are and spiritual gifted we may be. We need love. Money, status, position, and fame are all well and good, but in order to live the abundant life that Jesus talks about in (John 10:10) we need the spirit of love. Believe it or not love is one of the highest forms of spiritual warfare, this is why again Jesus tell us to love our enemies. Love is one of the spiritual gifts that God has given to everyone. In the mist of trouble and chaos most of us panic and forget all about the power of love, God and Jesus. Our lives would have less hurt, pain, and turmoil if we were to acknowledge and walk in love more often. But to walk in love it will take effort on our part. I'm not saying that it is easy either, but you can do it. Reflect and just think of those times when you operated or allowed God's love to operate through you. Think for a moment of a time of when you came out of trouble much quicker when you walked in love. If you just took a moment to realize how God's love rescued you right when it was about to turn for the worst, you would operate in love more often. Practices makes perfect, so practice your love walk today, right where you are. The more you practice walking in love, the better you will become at it.

Friend, if you want power for living, then check your love walk. Our love walk has a lot to do with everything that concerns us. If you are experiencing a lot of confusion, trouble, and failures look at your love walk because when all else fails, love will never fail. Love never fails, but we fail to love. We fail to operate in that which God commands to operate in from the beginning. How is your love walk? One of the most powerful men who have ever lived on the face of this earth was Jesus, God in the flesh. And Jesus had a serious love walk. To walk in love may not be easy, however, it is worth it. It may be hard at first, but it can become easier the more you learn to walk in it. Learn to walk in love one step at a time, one day, one moment, and one experience at a time and love will not fail you. Remember, God first calls us to love one another. So be very clear when the abuse comes, and an unpleasant situation finds your address, ask yourself this one question: What does love got to do with it? And the answer my friend is everything.

Peace and Love.

Put on love daily by praying and purposely walking in it.
Colossians 3:12-14

~

Hallelujah,
to the Lord God Almighty. Father
in the name of Jesus, I bless
your Holy name and I thank you
for your love. Today may I abide in
and walk in your perfect love, toward
you, others, and myself. Where
I am weak strengthen me
with your love and where
I am strong help me to
share your love.
AMEN.

~

V. Augustusel

Dear Friend, in order to possess the God kind of love discussed in this book, it is my belief that one must first come to know and understand our heavenly Father through a personal relationship with His Son, Jesus Christ. And the only way one can have this love relationship is to accept Jesus Christ as your personal Lord and Savior. You can do this by first believing that Jesus Christ is Lord. Then confess and purposely turn from a life of sin, death, and damnation. Surrender your life to God by praying this simple prayer, and allow Him to fill you with His Holy Spirit.

Father, in the name of Jesus, I recognize and acknowledge that I am a sinner. I now repent and purposely turn from a life of sin, death and destruction. I confess with my mouth and believe in my heart that Jesus Christ is Lord, and that you raised him from the dead. I invite you Lord Jesus to come into my life, and fill me with your love. Thank you for saving me. Amen. (Romans 10:9, 10)

Welcome to the family. Now that you have prayed and confessed the prayer, I pray that you will follow these simple instruction that will help you develop a strong love walk:

1. Pray, study, and obey God's word daily. Be joyful and purposely walk in love. (II Timothy 3:16) (I Thessalonians 5:16-18)

2. Find a good Bible believing church and join. Be faithful, and committed in a local church. Don't let nothing or no one turn you back. (Hebrews 10:25) Get baptized by water (Matthew 3:6) Pray and ask the Holy Spirit to baptize you in the spirit with the evidence of speaking in tongues (Acts 2:3-4)

3. Remember that God's love will never fail you. (John 3:16) (II Corinthians 3:8) If you fall in your daily walk with God, remember His love, get back up, repent, and keep walking with Him. (I John 3) (I John 4)

BIBLIOGRAPHY

Books, Articles, Documents

Benokraitis, Nijole V. *Marriages and Families: Changes, Choices, and Constraints*. 2nd. Edition. Upper Saddle River, NJ: Prentice Hall, Inc. 1993, 1996.

Bowden, John Richardson, Alan ed. *The Westminster Dictionary of Christian Theology*. Philadelphia, PA. The Westminster Press, 1983.

Webster's II New College Dictionary. Houghton Mifflin Co. 1995.

Websites

The New Testament Greek Lexicon www.Studylight.org.

The Old Testament Hebrew Lexicon www.Studylight.org.

Printed in the United States
35988LVS00004BA/112